Sonata III.

GEORGE FRIDERIC HANDEL

Transcribed by
Richard E. Powell

TROMBONE

PIANO

TROMBONE

PIANO

Allegro ♩ =112

4

[20]

SS-827

[45]

[50]

rit.

rit.

Trombone

Trombone

Baritone
or
Bb Trumpet

Baritone
or
Bb Trumpet

Baritone
or
B♭ Trumpet

Sonata III.

Trombone

Sonata III.

GEORGE FRIDERIC HANDEL
Transcribed by
Richard E. Powell

TROMBONE

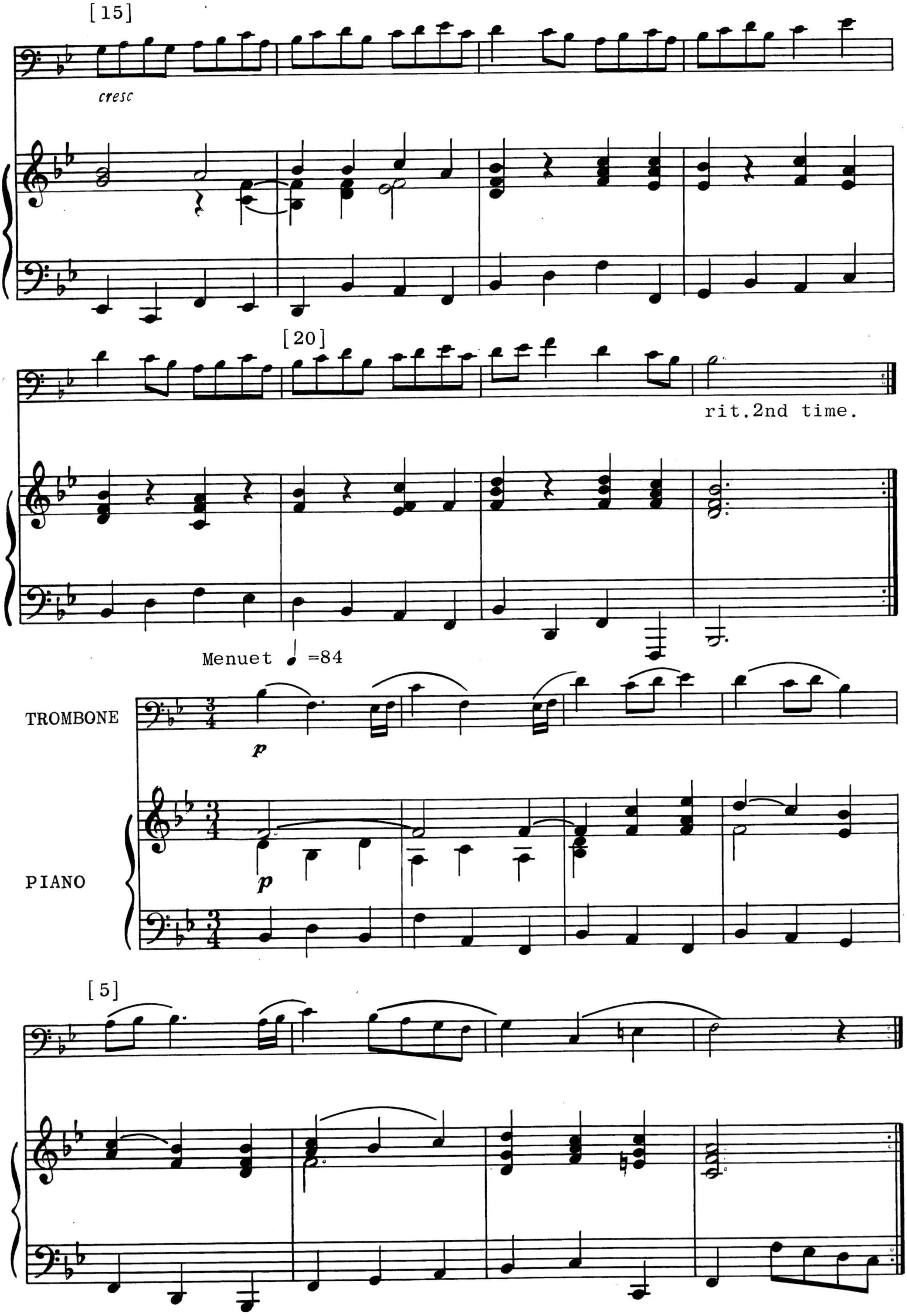
[15]
cresc
[20]
rit.2nd time.
Menuet ♩=84
TROMBONE
p
PIANO
p
[5]

SELECTED TROMBONE SOLOS AND STUDIES

Trombone Etudes and Instruction

GILLIS, LEW
B214	20 Etudes For Bass Trombone	HL3770297
B224	70 Progressive Studies for the Modern Bass Trombonist	HL3770307

A collection designed to assist the player/student in moving from the tenor trombone to the bass trombone including valve positions and development of pedal notes required for today's bass trombone repertoire. Includes: 60 studies in the use of F attachment; 10 studies in pedal notes; circle of keys scale studies.

HAINES, HARRY
B329TBN	Division Of Beat, Bk. 2	HL3770492
B497TBN	Rhythm Master, Beginning Bk. 1	HL3770819
B502TBN	Rhythm Master, Intermediate Bk. 2	HL3770841

HAINES, HARRY
Rhodes, Tom
B323TBN	Division Of Beat, Bk. 1a	HL3770466
B378TBN	Division Of Beat, Bk. 1b	HL3770576

HOFFMAN, EARL
B272	The Trigger Trombone	HL3770385

IRONS, EARL
B418	27 Groups Of Exercises	HL3770623

MARSTELLER, ROBERT
B237	Advanced Slide Technique	HL3770339
B268	Basic Routines	HL3770381

A volume of calisthenic exercises compiled to assist in the muscle development used in playing the trombone. Exercises are broken into four sections: (1)Attack and tome placement; (2) Slow Slurs; (3) Flexibility; (4) Scales and Arpeggios

PAUDERT, ERNST
Howey, Henry
B332	24 Studies	HL3770499

UBER, DAVID
B284	30 Etudes In The Bass And Tenor Clefs, Bk. 1	HL3770403
B286	30 Etudes In The Bass And Tenor Clefs, Bk. 2	HL3770404

UBER, DAVID
Donald Knaub
B335	30 Studies for Bass Trombone	HL3770502

VICTOR/ BIERSCHENK
Victor, John
B354TBN	Symphonic Band Technique	HL3770537

Trombone Solo with Keyboard

BACH, J.S.
Thomas Beversdorf
SS48	Haste, Ye Shepherds	HL3774108

BELLSTEDT, HERMANN
arr. Thurston/Simon
SS371	Napoli (trombone/euphonium)	HL3774006

Napoli is perhaps the most famous solo by Sousa arranger and cornet virtuoso 19th Century Hermann Bellstedt. Conceived as a theme and variations on a wildly popular 19th Century song, this edition by Bellstedt's student and Sousa band successor Frank Simon remains the one most performed today. This edition for trombone and euphonium by Tommy Fry comes with both bass and treble clef barts.

CORELLI, ARCANGELO
Powell, Richard
SS841	Prelude And Minuet	HL3774508

EWAZEN, ERIC
SU450	Ballade for Bass or Tenor Trombone (reduction)	HL3776369

Ballade for Bass or Tenor Trombone is based on an earlier work for clarinet and string orchestra. This arrangement was written for Charles Vernon of the Chicago Symphony in 1996, who later recorded the work on Albany Records (Troy 479). Comes with separate bass and tenor trombone parts. Duration ca. 12'.

SU339	Concerto No. 1 for Trombone (Sonata for Trombone)	HL3776236

Completed in the Spring of 1993, Ewazen's Sonata for Trombone was commissioned by Michael Powell who premiered the work at the Aspen Music Festival and recorded it on Cala Records. Later orchestra and band arrangements followed, both of which feature an added cadenza and are available separately from the publisher. Duration ca. 18', Grade 5.

FAURE, GABRIEL-URBAIN
Robert Marsteller
ST88	Elegie	HL3775723

GAUBERT, PHILIPPE
SS167	Morceau Symphonique	HL3773773

GEORGE, THOM RITTER
ST506	Sonata	HL3775220

GIFFELS, ANN
SS185	Sonata	HL3773792

HANDEL, GEORGE FRIDERIC
Fitzgerald, Bernard R.
ST755	Aria From Saul	HL3775563

HANDEL, GEORGE FRIDERIC
Powell, Richard
SS827	Sonata No. 3	HL3774492

HOFFMAN, EARL
ST93	The Big Horn	HL3775795
ST100	Trigger Treat (bass trombone)	HL3774692

MOZART, WOLFGANG AMADEUS
SS547	Concert Rondo, K371	HL3774185

MOZART, WOLFGANG AMADEUS
Powell, Richard
SS842	Arietta And Allegro, K109B/8 K3	HL3774509

SCHUDEL, THOMAS
SU289	An Angel Looked Over	HL3776169

SENAILLE, JEAN BAPTISTE
Arr. Leonard Falcone
SS563	Allegro Spiritoso	HL3774203

SOLOMON, EDWARD
SU135	Departure	HL3775956
ST128	Dramatique (bass trombone)	HL3774713
SU358	Slip Up Polka	HL3776257

UBER, DAVID
ST241	Ballad of Enob Mort	HL3774856
ST615	Rhapsody in F Minor	HL3775371

WALKER, GEORGE
S231001	Concerto for Trombone (piano reduction)	HL40208

An essential 20th-Century American work for Trombone. Recorded by Christian Lindbergh.

WHITE, DONALD
SS765	Sonata	HL3774428

Exclusively distributed by HAL•LEONARD CORPORATION

Questions/ comments? info@laurenkeisermusic.com